THE BOOK OF
CRAFTS

Memoria Press
Classical Core Curriculum

Second Grade

Lauren Arnwine

MEMORIA PRESS
www.MemoriaPress.com

THE BOOK OF CRAFTS
Memoria Press Classical Core Curriculum

SECOND GRADE
Lauren Arnwine

ISBN #978-1-61538-865-3

First Edition © 2017 Memoria Press

Illustrated by Jessica Osborne

CONTENTS

SUPPLY LIST

- [ ] Acrylic paint (various colors)
- [ ] Bottlecaps (12)
- [ ] Box (small)
- [ ] Brown paper bag
- [ ] Brown sugar or sand
- [ ] Buttons
- [ ] Cans (empty)
- [ ] Cardstock
- [ ] Cinnamon
- [ ] Circle sticker
- [ ] Clear lay film, 5" x 3.5" (overhead projector film)
- [ ] Clothespins
- [ ] Construction paper (various colors)
- [ ] Cotton balls
- [ ] Cotton swabs
- [ ] Craft sticks, miniature
- [ ] Crepe paper streamers (red, white, or blue)
- [ ] Crinkle-cut (brown)
- [ ] Cupcake liner
- [ ] Egg carton
- [ ] Felt (red, green, brown, white)
- [ ] File folder
- [ ] Fishing line
- [ ] Flour
- [ ] Foam bowl
- [ ] Foam cup, small
- [ ] Fuzzy balls (orange)
- [ ] Gathered leaves, flowers, sticks, rocks
- [ ] Glitter
- [ ] Glue (liquid & stick)
- [ ] Googly eyes

- [ ] Hole punch
- [ ] Hot glue
- [ ] Hot glue gun
- [ ] Iron
- [ ] Kid's sewing needle
- [ ] LED electric tealight
- [ ] Magazine clippings (something with underwater creatures like *Kid's National Geographic*)
- [ ] Markers
- [ ] Needle and thread
- [ ] Newspaper
- [ ] Paintbrushes
- [ ] Paper (white)
- [ ] Paper fastener
- [ ] Paper plates
- [ ] Paper towel
- [ ] Paper towel roll
- [ ] Pen
- [ ] Pencil
- [ ] Photos (from a child's trip out of state/country, to a museum, to grandma's house, etc.)
- [ ] Pipe cleaners (black, orange, brown, white or silver)
- [ ] Planting soil
- [ ] Plastic covering (i.e., bread, newspaper bag) or plastic wrap
- [ ] Popcorn
- [ ] Popsicle sticks
- [ ] Ribbon
- [ ] Ribbon candy
- [ ] Rubberbands
- [ ] Salt
- [ ] Scissors

- [ ] Seeds (apple, pumpkin, packet)
- [ ] Shoebox
- [ ] Stickers
- [ ] Straws
- [ ] String
- [ ] Tape
- [ ] Tissue paper (white, red)
- [ ] Toilet paper rolls
- [ ] Twine
- [ ] Water
- [ ] Wax paper
- [ ] Wooden "boy" pieces from craft store (2)
- [ ] Yarn (red)

INTRODUCTION

The creative arts are an essential part of the primary school education. By using the activities in this book, you can reinforce number and letter recognition, strengthen fine-motor skills, and foster creativity and confidence.

This book is intended to be a supplement to the Second Grade curriculum. The best way to work through these craft activities is to begin with reading all directions (which are directed to the teacher) thoroughly and assembling any supplies you will need to complete the project. Please note that some activities require adult help, and several of the crafts contain small items.

While the crafts in this book have been carefully chosen to promote skill growth and coordination, the most important component is fun. Enjoy each of your creations and the time spent with your child making them!

JOHNNY APPLESEED
Apple Pocket

Supplies:

☐ Apple template   ☐ Scissors

☐ Felt (red, green, and brown)   ☐ Apple seeds

☐ Yarn (red)   ☐ Liquid glue

☐ Kid's sewing needle

Teacher Guidelines:

1. Cut out apple template.

2. Trace and cut template twice out of red felt.

3. Have child cut a small leaf from green felt and stem from brown felt.

4. Hold both sides of apples together and puncture holes or cut slits around ¾ of the apple, leaving the top blank.

5. Cut about a foot of red yarn and lace onto child's needle with a knot on the end.

6. Have the child weave the yarn apple pocket together and tie off at the end.

7. Glue leaf and stem onto the front of the apple pocket.

8. Have child place apple seeds into apple pocket.

THE BOY WHO DREW BIRDS
Bird in Nest

Supplies:

- [ ] Bird template
- [ ] Construction paper (orange and desired color for bird)
- [ ] Crinkle-cut (brown)
- [ ] Cupcake liner
- [ ] Fishing line
- [ ] Liquid glue
- [ ] Googly eyes
- [ ] Yarn

Teacher Guidelines:

1. Cut out bird template, then trace onto construction paper and cut out to make the bird's body (OR just have child color template).
2. Cut out three small triangles from orange construction paper for bird's feet and beak.
3. Have child glue googly eyes and beak onto the head.
4. Cut two small pieces of yarn for legs and glue two remaining triangles on the end for feet.
5. Have child fill cupcake liner with brown crinkle-cut for the bird's nest.
6. Take a small piece of fishing line and tie around one of the bird's yarn legs to represent John Audubon's tracking method.
7. Set the bird inside his nest.

MCELLIGOT'S POOL
Tin Can Pool

Supplies:

- ☐ Glue stick
- ☐ Construction paper (blue, 4" x 8.5" strip)
- ☐ Construction paper (brown)
- ☐ 1 empty food can (clean)

- ☐ Magazine clippings (something with underwater creatures like *Kid's National Geographic*)
- ☐ Tape or glue
- ☐ Scissors

Teacher Guidelines:

1. Glue strip of blue construction paper around can.

2. Have child use brown construction paper to make a sign for "McElligot's Pool" and tape or glue onto the can.

3. Use magazines to cut out and put together items child thinks would be in McElligot's pool. Examples:
   - octopus wearing a hat
   - fish wearing tennis shoes
   - fish drinking water bottle

4. Have child arrange and glue cut-outs onto can.

THE MONKEY AND THE CROCODILE

Supplies:

- ☐ Scissors
- ☐ Pencil
- ☐ Liquid glue
- ☐ Googly eyes

Part 1: Crocodile

- ☐ Crocodile template
- ☐ Construction paper (green)
- ☐ White paper
- ☐ Clothespin

Part 2: Monkey & Mango Tree

- ☐ Monkey & mango tree template
- ☐ Construction paper (green, light brown, and dark brown)
- ☐ 3 pipe cleaners (brown)
- ☐ Fuzzy balls (orange)
- ☐ Empty paper towel roll
- ☐ Tape

Teacher Guidelines:

Part 1: Crocodile

1. Cut out crocodile templates and trace onto corresponding colors of construction paper. Have child cut out shapes from construction paper.
2. Glue green triangles onto the middle of the white triangles.
3. Draw zigzag lines on the white triangles around the border of the green triangles, then cut them out to form teeth.
4. Have child glue both finished sides onto the clothespin, with both white sides facing the same way. The flat end should be glued to the end of the clothespin that you squeeze, so that the mouth (the pointed end) opens.

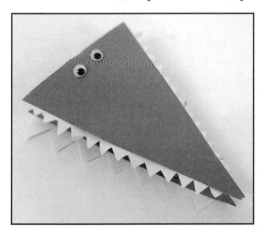

5. Glue googly eyes at the top of the crocodile's head.

Part 2: Monkey and Mango Tree

1. Cut out templates for the monkey. Trace and cut onto corresponding light and dark brown construction paper.
2. Glue small, light brown semi-circles onto monkey's ears and light brown oval onto his mouth.
3. Draw a smile onto the oval.
4. Glue googly eyes onto the monkey's head.
5. Glue monkey's head onto body.
6. Poke two holes on each side of the monkey's body (holes shown in square formation on template), for arm and leg holes.
7. Take two brown pipe cleaners and wrap them around paper towel holder and into the holes on the monkey.
8. Fold pipe cleaners down to secure, then cut remainder off.
9. Take third brown pipe cleaner and wrap around your finger to make a curly tail. Then tape it to the paper towel holder under the monkey's body.
10. Cut out mango leaf template and trace and cut out 5 times from green construction paper.
11. Tape ends of all 5 leaves together in a star formation. Then tape the cener of the star formation to the top of your tree.
12. Glue orange, fuzzy balls (mangoes) at the top of the paper towel holder, underneath leaves.

THE ANT AND THE ELEPHANT
Egg Carton Ant

Supplies:

☐ 3 connected holes from (non-plastic) egg carton

☐ Acrylic paint (black)

☐ Googly eyes

☐ Pipe cleaners (black, about 3)

Teacher Guidelines:

1. Begin with child painting egg carton black. Let dry.

2. Child then glues googly eyes onto front of ant's head.

3. Cut 2 antennas from pipe cleaners (about 1″). Stick them into the top of the ant's head (just poke pipe cleaner through) and bend tops down.

4. Cut remaining pipe cleaners into 6 equal pieces for legs.

5. Stick 3 legs into each side of the middle of the ant's body and bend them down to support ant.

ONE MORNING IN MAINE
Popsicle Boat

Supplies:

- ☐ Construction paper (brown)
- ☐ 30 regular popsicle sticks
- ☐ 8 miniature craft sticks
- ☐ Liquid glue
- ☐ Hot glue gun and hot glue (*adult use only)
- ☐ Acrylic paint or crayons

Teacher Guidelines:

1. Begin by having child paint or color the popsicle sticks before assembling. (If painting, set aside to dry completely.)

2. To build the sides of your boat, you are going to make 4 walls. Each wall needs 2 mini craft sticks and 7 regular popsicle sticks.

3. Lay 7 popsicle sticks horizontally, flat on your surface, stacked so the long sides touch. Have child glue a mini craft stick vertically on the ends at both sides. Repeat until all 4 sides are built.

4. Assemble the boat by hot gluing two sides together at an angle, and the other two sides at the same angle. Then glue both sets together to make the row boat. Result should be more of a diamond shape than a square.

5. Hot glue the remaining two popsicle sticks onto the side of the boat for oars. Start at the top of where the boat's sides meet, and angle them down to the ground.

6. Place boat on brown construction paper to trace outline. Cut and paste onto bottom of boat.

AMOS & BORIS
Foam Cup Whale

Supplies:

☐ Foam cup, small
(12 oz. used in example)

☐ Acrylic paint (blue)

☐ 3 pipe cleaners (white or silver)

☐ Construction paper (blue)

☐ Glue

☐ Tail/fin template

Teacher Guidelines:

1. Begin by having child paint entire outside of foam cup blue. Let dry.

2. Cut 2 pipe cleaners into thirds and 1 pipe cleaner into fourths.

3. Turn cup upside down.

4. Have child curl the tops of pipe cleaners down into circle shapes and stick into center of the top of the cup at various heights. Make all the curls face the same direction.

5. Have child glue googly eyes to bottom rim of cup.

6. Cut out tail and fin templates. Trace shapes onto blue construction paper and cut out.

7. Have child glue fins onto sides of cup and tail onto back/bottom.

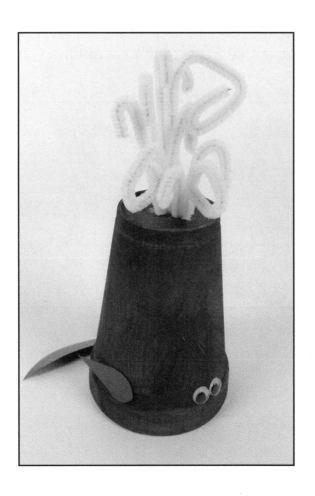

CINDERELLA
Mouse Clock

Supplies:

☐ 1 googly eye
☐ 1 small circle sticker
☐ Mouse template

☐ 2 inches of yarn
☐ Paper plate
☐ 1 paper fastener

Teacher Guidelines:

1. Turn plate upside down and write numbers around outer rim for the clock.

2. Cut out mouse template. Have child color body gray and ear pink.

3. Have child glue ear to the top of the mouse body, and glue yarn tail to back of the mouse. Attach googly eye.

4. Place mouse nose in center of plate, and poke fastener through mouse nose and plate. Fold down fastener ends on other side. Attach a small circle sticker on top of the fastener as the mouse nose.

MAYBELLE THE CABLE CAR
Cracker Box Cable Car

Supplies:

☐ Small empty box (cracker box used in example)

☐ Construction paper (yellow)

☐ Markers

☐ Plastic straw

☐ Yarn

☐ Tape

Teacher Guidelines:

1. Wrap your box in yellow construction paper as if you are gift-wrapping a present.

2. Have child draw on the wrapped box to make it look like a cable car.

3. Cut straw in fourths. Tape 2 parts to the top of the car side by side. (If you have a bigger/heavier box, tape remaining 2 straw parts to the bottom as well, for additional support.)

4. Help child thread a long string of yarn through each straw.

5. Tape the ends of the yarn to sturdy walls or surfaces.

6. Child can now drive cable car along the yarn.

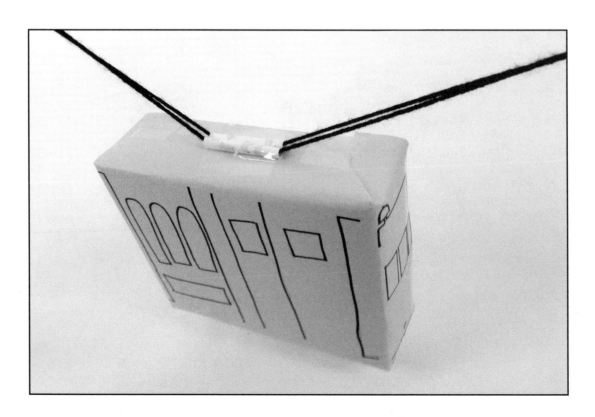

THE FIVE CHINESE BROTHERS
Shoebox Ocean Floor

Supplies:

☐ Shoebox

☐ Paper towel

☐ Liquid glue

☐ Brown sugar or sand

☐ Things your child can collect around the house or outside to go on the bottom of their ocean.

Teacher Guidelines:

1. If your shoebox does not have a plain white inside, you might want to cover sides (not bottom) with white paper.

2. Squirt some liquid glue along the bottom of the shoebox. Next, take the paper towel and spread the glue around the entire bottom of the shoebox.

3. Have the child quickly sprinkle brown sugar or sand over the wet glue. They can use as much or as little as they desire. Shake box gently to spread over entire surface. Let dry.

4. The child can now add gathered items to their ocean floor (i.e., seashells, rocks, fish toys, grass, plants, or treasure).

WEE GILLIS
Bagpipes

Supplies:

- ☐ 1 piece of felt (red, green, or brown)
- ☐ Plastic straw
- ☐ Needle and thread (for adult use)
- ☐ Yarn
- ☐ Tape

Teacher Guidelines:

1. Cut circle in felt about 6″ in diameter in desired color for bagpipes.

2. Have child draw lines to make a plaid pattern on felt (on one side).

3. Have child cut straw into 3 slightly uneven parts.

4. Have child place felt blank side up and tape 3 straw pieces to it (shortest to tallest) so they're sticking out of felt circle on top.

5. Thread needle. Weave wide stitches along entire outer edge of felt circle, then pull tight to draw together and form a bag. Cut string from needle and tie ends of string together.

6. Have child take the piece of yarn and wrap around each of the straws, weaving the yarn between each straw. Tie knot around outer straws to keep yarn in place.

THE THANKSGIVING STORY
Thankful Turkey

Supplies:

- ☐ Turkey template (circle, beak, gobbler)
- ☐ Construction paper (brown, red, yellow, and orange)
- ☐ 2 pipe cleaners (orange)
- ☐ 2 googly eyes
- ☐ Pen
- ☐ Scissors
- ☐ Liquid glue

Teacher Guidelines:

1. Trace child's hand three times, once each on yellow, red, and orange paper. Cut out.

2. Cut out the circle from the template and trace onto brown construction paper. Cut out.

3. Have child arrange 3 hand cutouts like feathers around brown circle and glue (this will be the back). Then flip over to the front and glue on googly eyes.

4. Cut out the beak and "gobbler" from the template and trace onto orange and red paper. Have child cut out and glue underneath googly eyes.

5. Have child write on turkey "feathers" things they are thankful for.

6. Starting at one end of an orange pipe cleaner, bend back into three 1" folds, making 3 toes. Wrap pipe cleaner around itself to stabilize and cut off remainder, leaving a little extra to attach to turkey. Repeat for the second foot.

7. Bend excess up and tape to back of turkey so toes extend forward. Let dry fully before standing.

LUCY'S CHRISTMAS
Popcorn and Candy Gifts

Supplies:

☐ Tissue paper (red)   ☐ Ribbon candy

☐ Popcorn   ☐ Ribbon

Teacher Guidelines:

1. Pop popcorn.

2. Have child put some popcorn and ribbon candy into center of tissue paper and wrap up. Tie with ribbon.

3. Have child give to family, friends, and neighbors as Christmas presents like Lucy gave to her friends.

THE CHRISTMAS MIRACLE OF JONATHAN TOOMEY
Wooden Nativity Ornament

Supplies:

☐ Small strip of twine

☐ 2 wooden "boy" pieces from craft store

☐ Tape

☐ Hot glue gun and hot glue (*adult use only)

☐ Acrylic paints (baby-blue and gray, or black & blue mixed with white)

☐ 2 pieces of felt (white, ¾" x ¾")

Teacher Guidelines:

1. Wrap tape around wooden heads to keep paint off. Have child paint the bodies of one wooden piece gray and one blue. Let dry.

2. Hot glue one piece of felt onto Mary's head (gray wooden piece) as a hair covering.

3. Fold the other felt piece to look like a swaddled baby.

4. Tie twine around Joseph and Mary. Then tuck the folded felt piece in between the twine and wooden pieces so Mary and Joseph are holding baby Jesus.

*Pieces in image are enlarged to show detail.

THE VELVETEEN RABBIT
Rabbit Mobile

Supplies:

☐ Piece of string about 1 yard long (white or neutral color)

☐ Old newspaper or magazine

☐ Rabbit template

☐ Tape

Teacher Guidelines:

1. Cut out rabbit template and trace 4 times onto an old newspaper or magazine. Cut out shapes.

2. Lay string down and lay rabbits along it (ear to foot), spaced evenly.

3. Have child tape rabbits onto the string.

4. Hang up.

THE BIG SNOW
Hibernating Bear

Supplies:

- [ ] Liquid glue
- [ ] Scissors
- [ ] 2 paper plates
- [ ] Markers (brown and black)
- [ ] Pencil
- [ ] Construction paper (green)
- [ ] Piece of tissue paper (white, cut into squares)
- [ ] Paper fastener
- [ ] Tree and Bear template

Teacher Guidelines:

1. Cut out the tree template and trace onto green construction paper to make as many trees as child wants. Cut out shapes.

2. Draw a line in pencil vertically down the middle of trees. Starting from the outside edges, cut diagonally inward almost to the center line. Do this for right and left sides of each tree, creating the appearance of pine branches. Finish trees and set aside.

3. Have child cut out bear template and color bear with brown marker. Set aside.

4. Cut middle center out of one paper plate, about 5" in diameter. (Fold plate over to make first cut without cutting through the side.) Set aside for later.

5. On uncut paper plate, have child color a circle in the middle (about 4" in diameter) with black marker; glue bear on center.

6. Use the paper fastener to attach the cut-out center of the first paper plate to the top, center of the colored middle circle of the second (the "bear cave"), so that "cave" is entirely covered by the cutout.

7. Have child glue trees around the outside edges of paper plate where they desire.

8. For snow, have child glue tissue-paper squares to cover the remainder of the paper plate.

THE EMPEROR'S NEW CLOTHES
Decorative Shirt

Supplies:

- [ ] Shirt template
- [ ] White paper
- [ ] Scissors
- [ ] Markers
- [ ] Things to decorate with (stickers, buttons, etc.)
- [ ] String
- [ ] 2 clothespins

Teacher Guidelines:

1. Cut out shirt template; trace onto white paper and cut out (or just use template).
2. Have child write a memory verse or poem on it.
3. Decorate.
4. Hang on string using two clothespins and tape up onto the wall.

A PICTURE BOOK OF AMELIA EARHART
Clothespin Airplane

Supplies:

- ☐ Clothespin
- ☐ Mini craft stick
- ☐ 2 popsicle sticks
- ☐ Paint or markers
- ☐ Liquid glue

(You may need duplicate supplies if you want to make multiple airplanes!)

Teacher Guidelines:

1. Begin by having child color clothespin and craft sticks.

2. Help child glue one regular popsicle stick perpendicularly on top of clothespin about an inch away from the side that opens, and glue other popsicle stick parallel to the first onto the opposite side.

3. Help child glue mini craft stick on top of the clothespin about half an inch from opposite end.

SAINT VALENTINE
Valentine Card

Supplies:

- ☐ Pumpkin seeds
- ☐ Acrylic paint (yellow)
- ☐ Paintbrush
- ☐ Marker (green)
- ☐ Liquid glue
- ☐ Piece of cardstock or construction paper

Teacher Guidelines:

1. Begin by having child paint pumpkin seeds yellow. Set aside to dry. (you need 3 seeds per flower, for however many flowers you want)

2. Have child glue pumpkin seeds in shape of flower onto cardstock or construction paper (3 seeds per flower) to decorate the card.

3. Child can now draw green stems/leaves onto the paper beneath the glued flower.

4. Have child write a message on the card and sign "From Your Valentine."

GEORGE WASHINGTON'S BREAKFAST
George Washington Puppet

Supplies:

☐ Brown paper bag

☐ Cardstock (white)

☐ Presidential hat & bowtie template

☐ Construction paper (blue and yellow)

☐ Marker (black)

☐ Liquid glue

☐ 8 cotton balls

Teacher Guidelines:

1. Cut about a 5-inch circle out of white cardstock.

2. Have child glue circle onto bottom of paper bag, on flap (open side of bag will be bottom of puppet) and draw a face on Washington.

3. Cut out hat template and trace onto blue construction paper, and then cut out. Child can glue the hat onto the head of Washington.

4. Have child glue cotton balls on sides of Washington's head underneath his hat for his hair.

5. Cut out bowtie template and trace onto yellow construction paper, and then cut out. Color center knot black. Have child glue onto paper bag.

FAREWELL TO SHADY GLADE
Toilet Paper Roll Train

Supplies:

- ☐ 3 toilet paper rolls
- ☐ 12 bottlecaps
- ☐ Acrylic paint (3 colors)
- ☐ Paintbrush
- ☐ Scissors
- ☐ Hot glue gun and hot glue (*adult use only)
- ☐ Cotton ball
- ☐ Clothespin
- ☐ Yarn
- ☐ Hole punch

Teacher Guidelines:

1. Begin by having child paint each toilet paper roll a different color. Let dry.

2. Hot glue 4 bottlecaps on the sides of each toilet paper roll for wheels.

3. Cut a one inch slit in the top of the front train car near one end.

4. Open your clothespin and pinch cotton ball. Then stretch the cotton ball out so that it looks like steam. Insert bottom of clothespin into the roll with the cut slit on the top. This is your train engine.

5. Hole punch two holes on the top of the train engine, about half an inch apart, on the opposite end from the "smokestack." On the second train car, punch four holes on top, one set at the front and one at the back. On the third car, punch two holes on one end only.

6. Cut 2 strips of yarn. Have child thread a piece of yarn in the holes to connect the engine to the second car. Repeat to connect the second and third car.

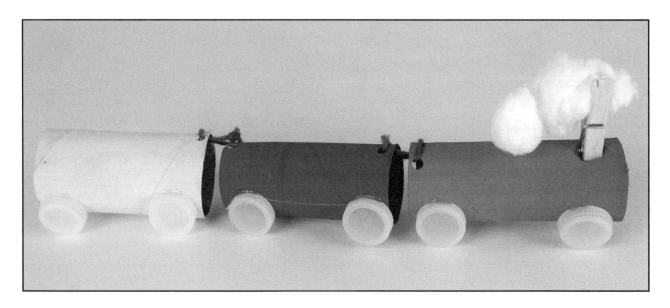

CYRUS THE UNSINKABLE SEA SERPENT
Paper Chain Sea Serpent

Supplies:

- ☐ Construction paper (2 different colors— we recommend greens & blues)
- ☐ Tape
- ☐ Googly eye
- ☐ Scissors
- ☐ Marker
- ☐ Liquid glue
- ☐ Sea serpent head template

Teacher Guidelines:

1. Take a piece of construction paper and fold in half (horizontally), then cut along fold. Then cut 8 strips from each half (make cuts along short edge). You should have 16 strips.

2. Take the first strip, make a loop, and tape closed. Take the next strip, loop through first loop, and tape closed. Continue until you've made a paper chain with all of the strips.

3. Cut out sea serpent head templates and trace onto two pieces of different-colored construction paper (head, same color as paper chain; spikes, a different color). Cut out shapes.

4. Have child glue spikes onto head, and then glue googly eye onto head.

5. Child can now draw a nostril and a smile.

6. Finally, have child glue head onto end of paper chain.

EMILY
Flower Bookmark

Supplies:

☐ Gathered leaves and flowers
☐ Wax paper

☐ Iron (*adult use only)
☐ Scissors

Teacher Guidelines:

1. Cut a strip of wax paper 14″ x 3″. Fold in half.

2. Have child gather flowers and leaves and then put inside the wax paper fold.

3. Iron the bookmark on medium heat until flowers are pressed and wax paper is sealed together.

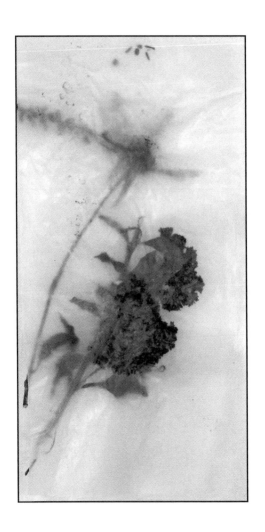

SAM, BANGS & MOONSHINE
Cat Toilet Paper Roll

Supplies:

- ☐ 3 pipe cleaners (black)
- ☐ Toilet paper roll
- ☐ Acrylic paint (black)
- ☐ White paper

- ☐ Markers (pink, yellow, black)
- ☐ Liquid glue
- ☐ Hot glue gun and hot glue (*adult use only)

Teacher Guidelines:

1. Begin by having child paint toilet paper roll black. Let dry.

2. Cut 2 small ovals and a small triangle out of white paper for a nose and eyes.

3. Have child color nose pink and color eyes yellow with black pupils.

4. Cut a black pipe cleaner in half. Poke into the back bottom of toilet paper roll for a tail. Curl the end slightly.

5. Take top of toilet paper roll and fold down in the middle on both sides. They should overlap to make two ears.

6. Have child glue on eyes and nose.

7. Cut remaining 2 pipe cleaners into 2-inch pieces. You'll need 6 pieces for whiskers. Hot glue 3 whiskers on each side of the nose. You may need to hot glue the tail on the inside of the toilet paper roll to stabilize it.

ISLAND BOY
Paper Plate Island

Supplies:

- ☐ 1 cup flour
- ☐ ¼ cup salt
- ☐ ½ cup water
- ☐ Cinnamon

- ☐ Paper plate
- ☐ Acrylic paint (blue)
- ☐ Sticks, leaves, rocks, etc. (gathered from nature)

Teacher Guidelines:

1. Begin by having child paint bottom section of paper plate blue (leave middle of plate blank for island). Set aside to dry.

2. Make homemade playdough.

   - Mix flour and salt.

   - Separately mix water and a pinch of cinnamon for color.

   - Then slowly mix everything together and knead mixture until everything is absorbed and you have a good consistency. You can add extra flour if playdough is too sticky.

3. Have child cover entire center of the plate with the playdough to make an island. It can be as thick or as thin as you desire.

4. Have child use gathered nature items to stick onto the island. Set aside to let playdough harden.

THE EASTER EGG
Egg Wreath

Supplies:

- ☐ Egg template (7 eggs)
- ☐ Scissors
- ☐ Liquid glue
- ☐ Paper plate
- ☐ Things to decorate (markers, glitter, stickers, etc.)
- ☐ Hole punch
- ☐ Ribbon

Teacher Guidelines:

1. Begin by having child cut eggs out of template.

2. Cut center out of paper plate, about 5 inches in diameter. (So you don't cut the side of the plate, fold the plate over to slit the center to start cutting.)

3. Trim outside of paper plate off so you have a ring about half an inch wide. This is the base of the wreath onto which you will glue the eggs.

4. Have child decorate eggs.

5. Child can now glue eggs onto paper-plate ring.

6. Hole punch top egg; tie a ribbon through the hole and hang.

PAUL REVERE'S RIDE
Lantern

Supplies:

- ☐ LED electric tealight
- ☐ Clear lay film, 5" x 3.5" (overhead projector transparency)
- ☐ Circle template
- ☐ Construction paper
- ☐ Tape
- ☐ String/twine
- ☐ Scissors
- ☐ Hole punch

Teacher Guidelines:

1. Cut film by measuring it around tealight for width, and measuring 3.5" for height.

2. Have child tape around tealight. Make sure bottom of tealight and bottom of film are flush.

3. Measure and cut a strip of construction paper that is the height of the tealight and that will fully wrap around the outside of tealight and clear film. Have child cut and tape around bottom of lantern. You may want to put a tape strip along the bottom of lantern to hold tealight in.

4. Cut out circle template and trace (or use a small cup to trace) on construction paper. Cut circle out. Cut a slit in the circle from edge to the middle. Then slightly overlap the circle where the slit is to form a shallow cone shape.

5. Help child hole punch a hole in each side of the lantern for handles, about 1 inch down from top of plastic, on opposite sides. Then, punch a hole on each side of the cone, about ½ inch from edge.

6. Thread string or twine through one hole in lantern, starting from outside. Pull through and thread through hole on opposite side. Thread one end of string up through one hole on underside of cone. Do the same for the other end of the string and tie a knot above cone. Slide cone down onto top of lantern and secure in place with tape.

VERDI
Paper Plate Snake

Supplies:

- ☐ Acrylic paint (green)
- ☐ Paintbrush
- ☐ Googly eyes
- ☐ Liquid glue
- ☐ Scissors
- ☐ Pencil
- ☐ Construction paper (2" x ½" strip, red)
- ☐ Paper plate

Teacher Guidelines:

1. Begin by having child paint plate green. Let dry.

2. Starting on the outside edge of paper plate, cut in a spiral inwards towards center of plate to make snake body (about one inch wide). Stop when you have a small circle in the center for the head. You may want to draw a line in the spiral shape for the child to cut along.

3. Have child glue googly eyes on head.

4. Cut red strip of paper. Cut a slit (triangle shape) out of one end of the strip to make the snake tongue. Have child the glue the tongue onto the bottom of the head so it looks like it's sticking out of the mouth.

5. Have the child decorate the rest of the snake body if desired.

THE GIFT OF THE TREE
Tree Painting

Supplies:

☐ Tree template

☐ Cotton swabs (2 handfuls)

☐ Rubberband

☐ Acrylic paints (white, blue, green, red, yellow, orange; can mix primary colors to get secondary colors)

Teacher Guidelines:

1. Photocopy tree template onto cardstock or tear/cut out page. The tree is going to exhibit all of the seasons, represented on each of the three main branches of the tree template. Have child paint the left branch green for spring and summer, the middle red, orange, and yellow for fall, and paint the right branch white or light blue to look like snow for winter.

2. Take a handful of cotton swabs and tie a rubber band around them. Have child dip in paint and dot the paint onto the tree.

3. After the child finishes one color, you can turn cotton swab bundle over and use the other side. You may need a couple bundles to paint entire tree. Let dry.

THE GARDENER
Egg Carton Garden

Supplies:

☐ Empty egg carton

☐ Planting soil

☐ Packet of seeds (flowers, vegetables, etc.)

☐ Plastic covering (i.e., bread or newspaper bag) or plastic wrap

☐ Water

Teacher Guidelines:

1. Cut top off of egg carton.

2. Have child fill bottom half of holes with soil.

3. Spread seeds.

4. Fill the remainder of holes up with soil to cover seeds.

5. Add water.

6. Place in sunshine.

7. If inside, place in plastic bag to preserve water inside egg carton (this is optional). Place in window to get sunlight. Water regularly.

A VISIT TO WILLIAM BLAKE'S INN
Scrapbook Suitcase

Supplies:

- [ ] Suitcase template
- [ ] 1 file folder
- [ ] Construction paper
- [ ] Liquid glue
- [ ] String
- [ ] Scissors
- [ ] Marker
- [ ] 3 or 4 photos from a child's trip out of state/country, to a museum, to grandma's house, etc.

Teacher Guidelines:

1. Cut file tab off the top of the folder so that it is even on top.

2. Cut out template and trace onto construction paper (suitcase handle x 2 and luggage tag). Have child cut shapes out.

3. Along outside of long edge that opens, have child glue suitcase handles, near top.

4. Cut 4 strips of construction paper that are about 1-1.5 inches in width and the length of the folder from handles to the bottom of the folder (at folded edge). Have child glue onto folder.

5. Have child write name on luggage tag. Cut slit in luggage tag and insert string. Tie onto one suitcase handle.

6. Open suitcase and child can glue photos inside.

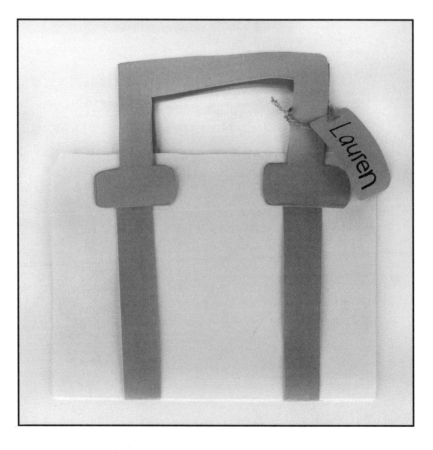

THE 4TH OF JULY STORY
Windcatcher

Supplies:

- ☐ Empty can (clean)
- ☐ Acrylic paints (red, white, or blue)
- ☐ Paintbrush
- ☐ Twine
- ☐ Crepe paper streamers (red, white, or blue)
- ☐ Hot glue gun and hot glue (*adult use only)

Teacher Guidelines:

1. Begin by having child paint can, including bottom. Let dry.

2. Child can decorate can with stars in patriotic colors, if desired.

3. Turn can upside down. Hot glue ends of twine onto each side of the bottom of the can to make a handle.

4. Have child cut streamer strips about two feet in length.

5. Use hot glue gun to glue streamers onto the other side of the can (open end). Glue them all the way around the inside of the can so they hang down and catch wind.

6. Hang up outside on porch or in a tree.

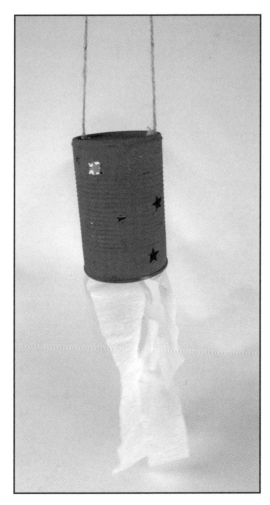

LUCY'S SUMMER
Lucy's Hat

Supplies:

☐ Paper plate

☐ Foam bowl

☐ Liquid glue

☐ Scissors

☐ Things to decorate hat (feathers, ribbon, flowers, stickers, poms, markers, pipe cleaners, etc.)

Teacher Guidelines:

1. Flip bowl upside down and use it to trace a circle on bottom of the paper plate. Cut out circle.

2. Glue bowl upside down on bottom of plate, covering hole.

3. Have child decorate hat.

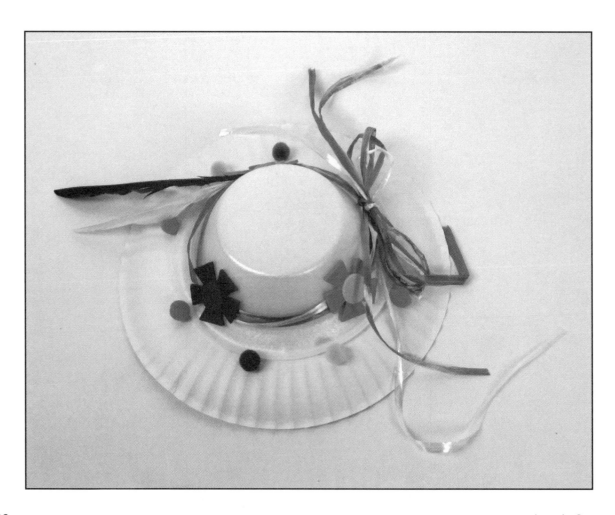

TEMPLATES

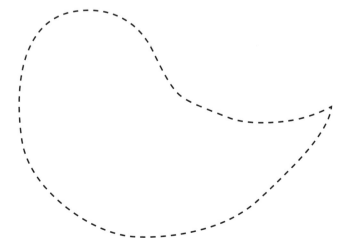

White

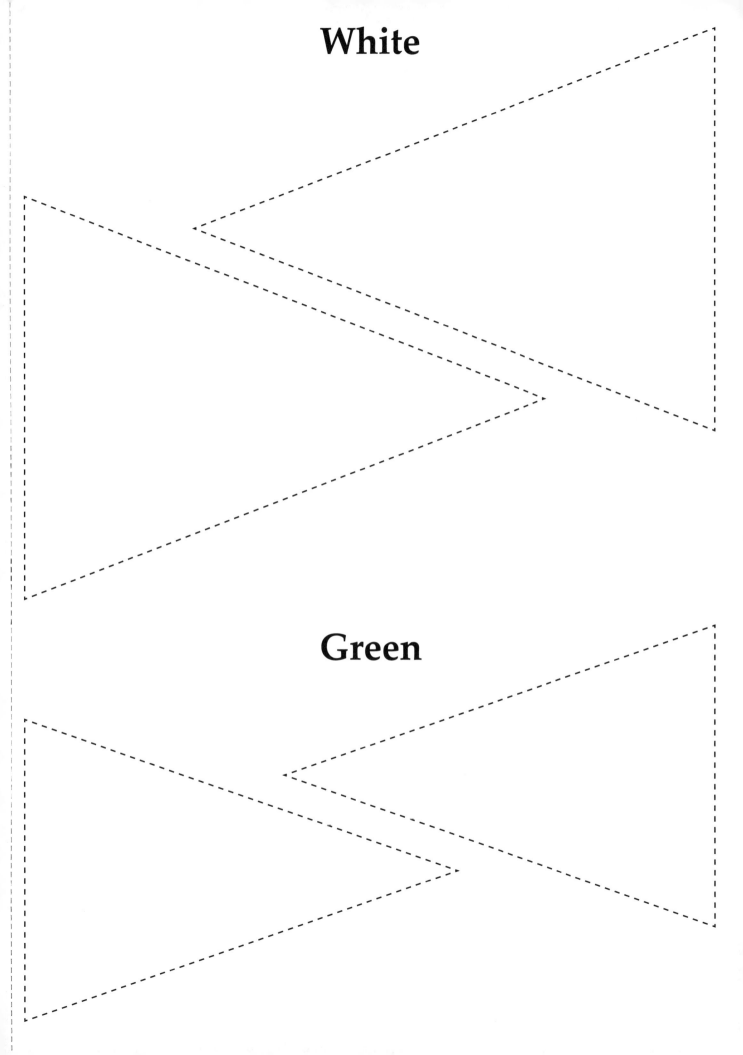

Green

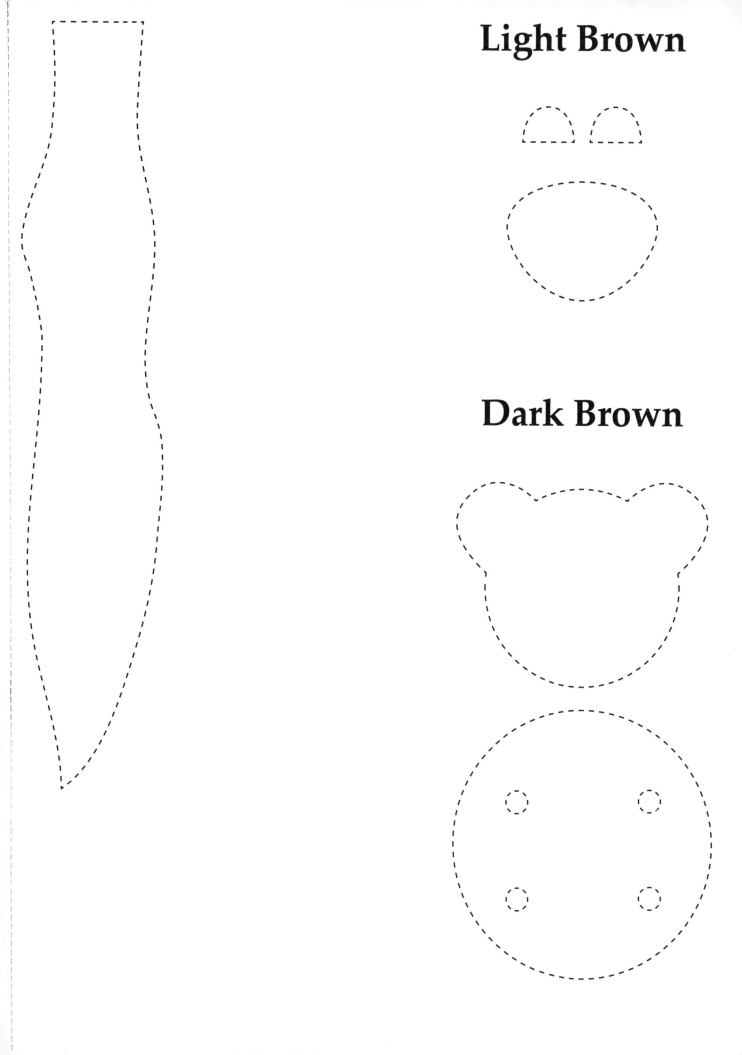

Light Brown

Dark Brown

The Monkey and the Crocodile (Monkey and mango tree template)

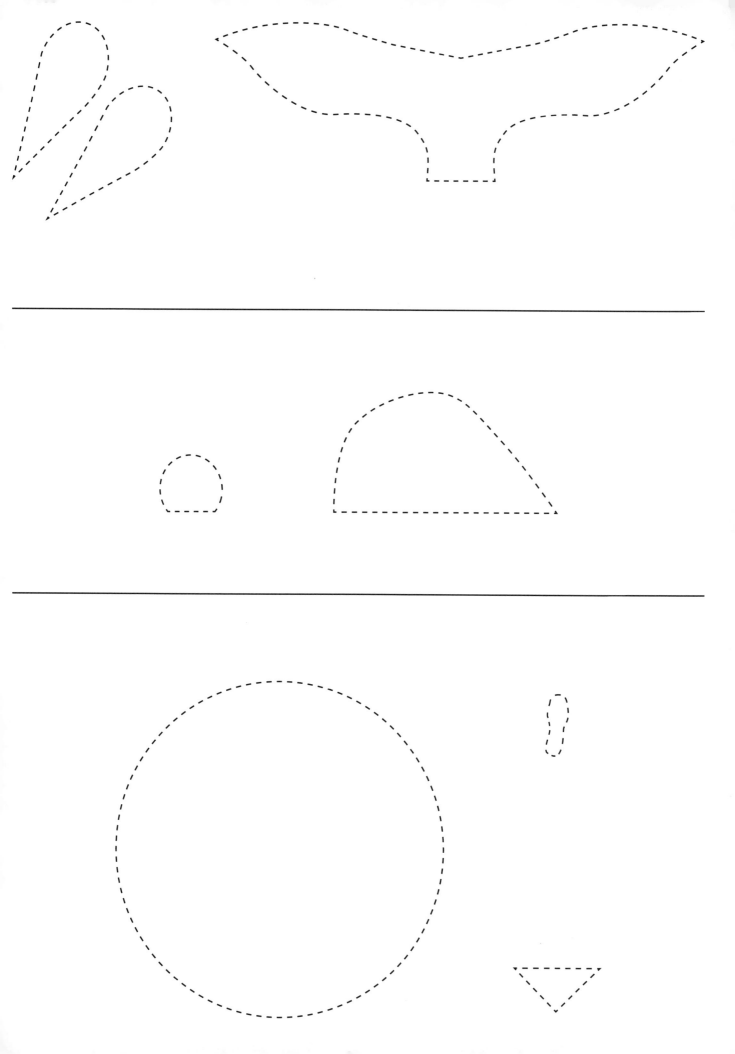

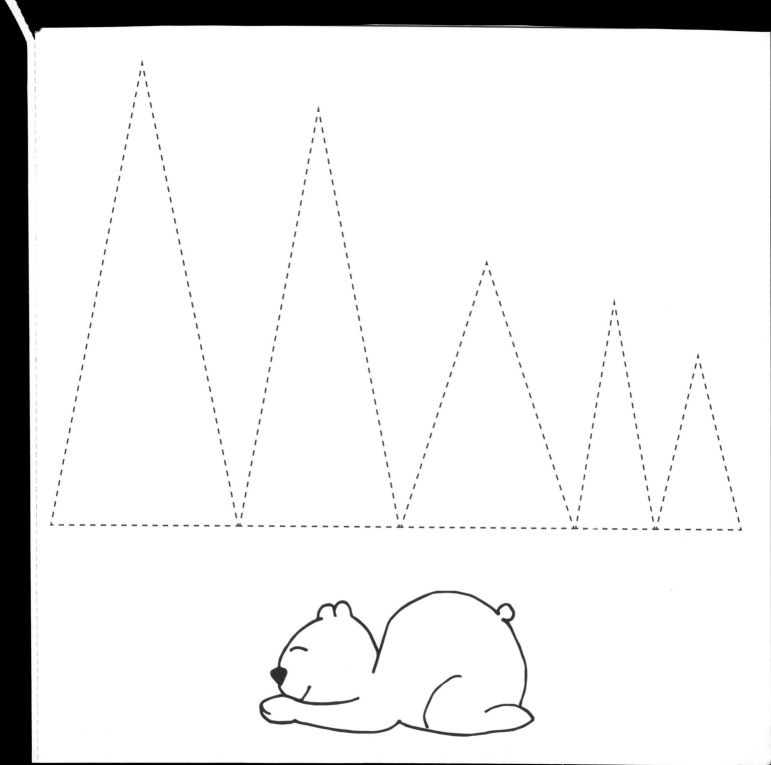

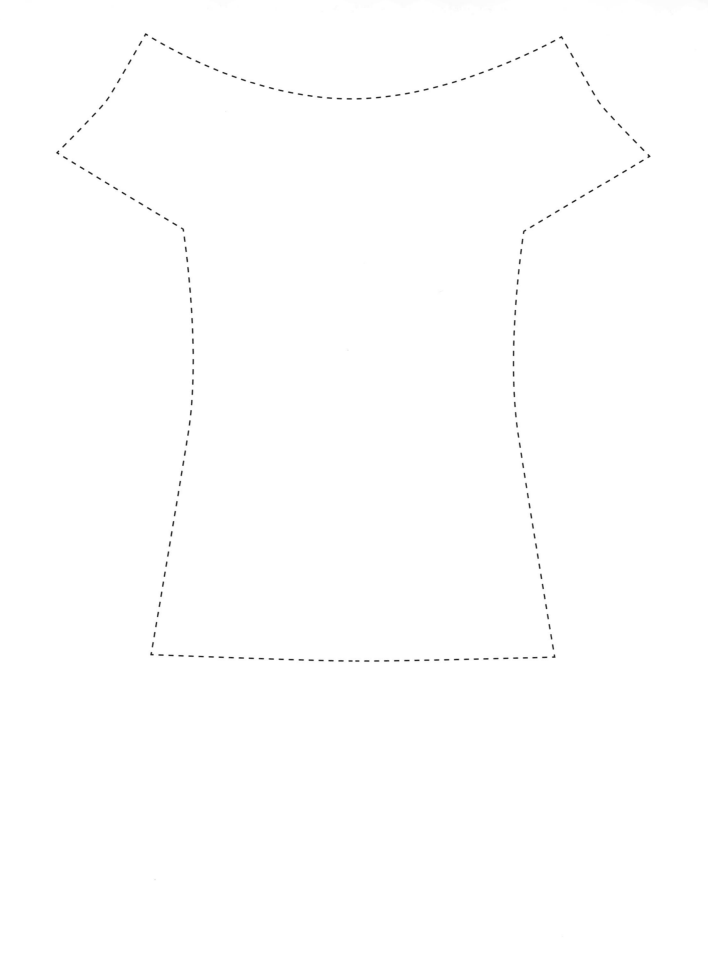

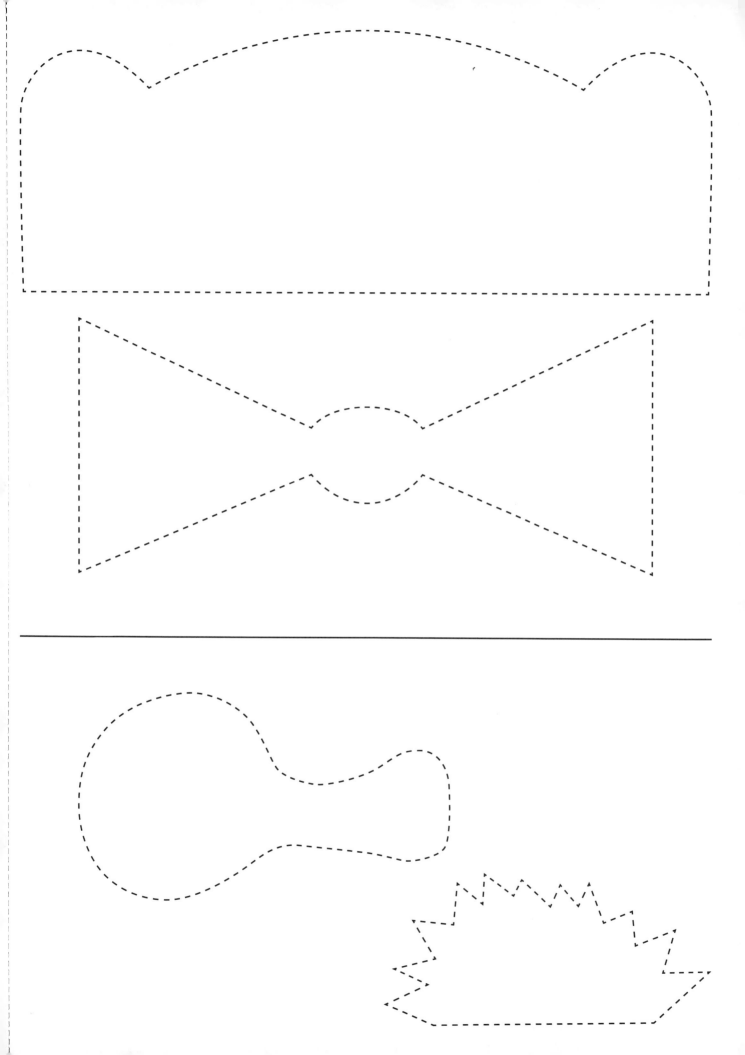

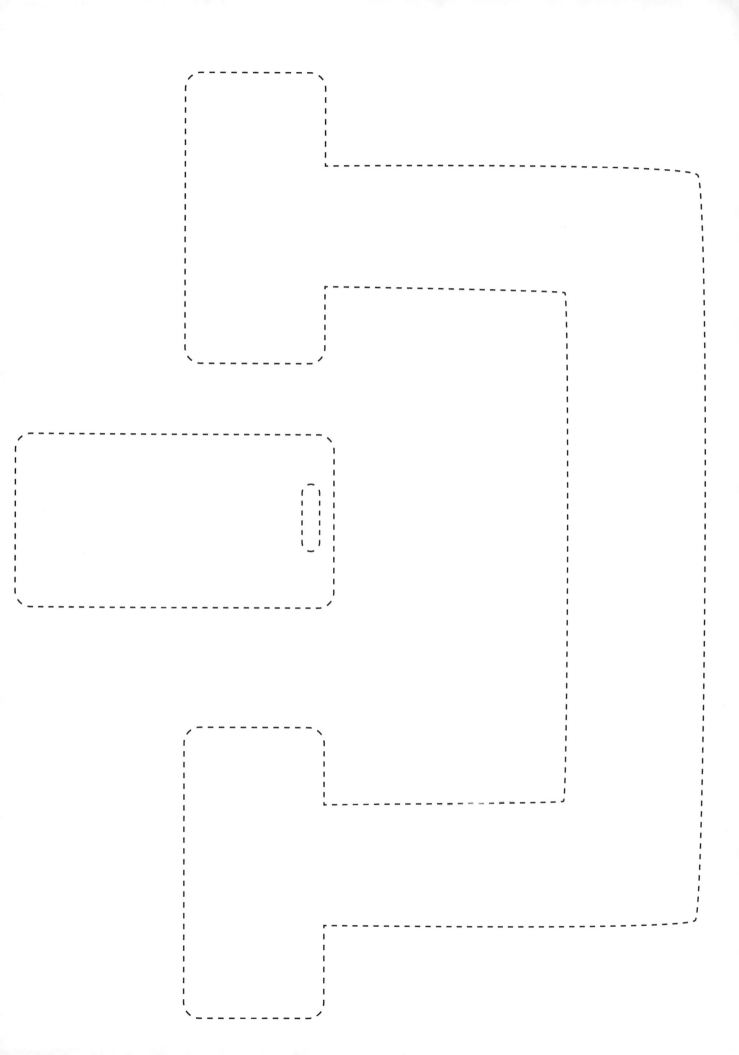